THE

ing

Noam Chomsky is the au——
influential political books, inclu——
Failed States, Interventions, What we —— ——, *Hopes and*
Prospects, Gaza in Crisis and *Making th* —— *uture,* all of which
are published by Hamish Hamilton/Penguin. He is an
Institute Professor (Emeritus) in the Department of Linguistics and Philosophy at MIT, and is widely credited with
having revolutionized modern linguistics.

Chomsky has supported the initiatives of the Occupy
movement from its first weeks. He lives in Lexington,
Massachusetts.

OCCUPY

NOAM CHOMSKY

PENGUIN BOOKS

PENGUIN BOOKS

Published by the Penguin Group
Penguin Books Ltd, 80 Strand, London WC2R 0RL, England
Penguin Group (USA) Inc., 375 Hudson Street, New York, New York 10014, USA
Penguin Group (Canada), 90 Eglinton Avenue East, Suite 700, Toronto, Ontario,
Canada M4P 2Y3 (a division of Pearson Penguin Canada Inc.)
Penguin Ireland, 25 St Stephen's Green, Dublin 2, Ireland
(a division of Penguin Books Ltd)
Penguin Group (Australia), 250 Camberwell Road, Camberwell, Victoria 3124,
Australia (a division of Pearson Australia Group Pty Ltd)
Penguin Books India Pvt Ltd, 11 Community Centre, Panchsheel Park,
New Delhi – 110 017, India
Penguin Group (NZ), 67 Apollo Drive, Rosedale, Auckland 0632, New Zealand
(a division of Pearson New Zealand Ltd)
Penguin Books (South Africa) (Pty) Ltd, Block D, Rosebank Office Park,
181 Jan Smuts Avenue, Parktown North, Gauteng 2193, South Africa

Penguin Books Ltd, Registered Offices: 80 Strand, London WC2R 0RL, England

www.penguin.com

First published in the United States of America by Zuccotti Park Press 2012
Published in Great Britain in Penguin Books 2012

009

Copyright © Noam Chomsky, 2012

Printed in Great Britain by Clays Ltd, St Ives plc

A CIP catalogue record for this book is available from the British Library

ISBN: 978-0-241-96401-9

www.greenpenguin.co.uk

MIX
Paper from
responsible sources
FSC www.fsc.org   FSC® C018179

Penguin Books is committed to a sustainable
future for our business, our readers and our planet.
This book is made from Forest Stewardship
Council™ certified paper.

CONTENTS

Art and Photography

Dedicated to the 6,705 people who have been arrested supporting Occupy to date, from the first 80 arrested marching in New York on September 24, 2011, to the woman arrested in Sacramento on March 6, 2012, for throwing flower petals. May our numbers swell and increase.*

---

* Torey Van Oot, "'Occupy' protester arrested for throwing flower petals in Capitol," *Sacramento Bee*, March 6, 2012.

EDITOR'S NOTE

"Occupy," says Noam Chomsky, "is the first major public response to thirty years of class war," a people-powered movement that began in New York City on September 17, 2011, and rapidly spread to thousands of locations worldwide. Although most of the original sites have been raided by police, by early 2012 the movement had already transitioned from occupying tent camps to occupying the national conscience.

In his talks, Chomsky points out that one of the movement's greatest successes has been simply to put the inequalities of everyday life on the national agenda, influencing reporting, public perception and language itself. Referencing a January 2012 Pew Research Center report on public perceptions of class conflict within the United States, Chomsky notes that inequalities in the country "have risen to historically unprecedented heights." The Pew study finds that about two-thirds of the U.S. population now believes there are "very strong" or "strong" conflicts between the rich and the poor—an increase of 19 percentage points since 2009.[*]

By early 2012 it had also become cliché to say that Occupy has changed the national conversation. It has done that, and it is important to acknowledge all the people who camped out, marched or went to jail to help make it happen. More than 6,705 people in 112 U.S. cities have been arrested as of this writing.[†] It is now commonplace to see not only increased coverage of the problems of income disparity, but also to regularly see newspaper articles with headlines that reflect the language of the movement. For example, on February 15, 2012, the *New York Times* published an article with the title, "Why Obama Will Embrace the 99 Percent."[‡] Making headlines is not the movement's goal, but the word choice indicates that the narrative can be changed—and altering the narrative is a necessary victory toward transforming everything else.

The plight of those without resources, those without a voice, those without access to power,

---

[*] Rich Morin, "Rising Share of Americans See Conflict Between Rich and Poor," Pew Research Center, January 11, 2012.

[†] OccupyArrests.com posts a running total of how many Occupy protesters have been arrested since September 17, 2011, and when and where in the United States the arrests took place.

[‡] Nate Silver, "Why Obama Will Embrace the 99 Percent," *New York Times*, published online February 15, 2012.

traditionally ignored, has now become the focus of greater national attention and widespread indignation. Their stories are being told, and anyone who can read and understand cannot help but deplore the cruelties endured by millions of people in an economy that for decades has been shaped and coded to serve the rich. Another recent example: The *New York Times* recently published a front-page story about an elderly couple in Dixfield, Maine, who had fallen behind on paying their heating bills. When, during the dead of winter, their back debt hit around $700, the oil company cut them off, knowing that doing so might literally kill two people. The oil man said he "agonized over his decision," and when he got off the phone with the couple he thought to himself, "Are these people going to be found frozen?"*

In the same issue, just a few pages later, appeared a column discussing multimillionaire Mitt Romney's statement that he was "not concerned about the very poor" because there is a "safety net" for them. The writer responds to Romney's assurance with these words: "Where to begin? First, a report from the Center on Budget and Policy Priorities last month pointed

---

* Dan Barry, "In Fuel Oil Country, Cold That Cuts to the Heart," *New York Times*, February 3, 2012.

out that Romney's budget proposals would take a chainsaw to that safety net."*

How did we in the United States get to this point? "It's not Third World misery," says Chomsky, "but it's not what it ought to be in a rich society, the richest in the world, in fact, with plenty of wealth around, which people can see, just not in their pockets." And Chomsky credits Occupy for helping to bring these issues to the fore. "You can say that it's now almost a standard framework of discussion. Even the terminology is accepted. That's a big shift."

Driving the shift are Occupy's relentless and increasingly creative actions in hundreds of cities, including occupying foreclosed homes and disrupting auctions where people's stolen homes are sold off to the highest bidder.† These actions not only expose the heartlessness and inhumanity of the system; they offer meaningful solidarity to those being crushed by it.

Chomsky speaks to the many options and opportunities that exist to change the system, and he points to examples in which the movement's

---

* Charles M. Blow, "Romney, the Rich and the Rest," *New York Times*, February 3, 2012, citing Richard Kogan and Paul N. Van de Water, "Romney Budget Proposals Would Require Massive Cuts in Medicare, Medicaid, and Other Nondefense Spending," Center on Budget and Policy Priorities, revised February 16, 2012.

† Allison Kilkenny, "Report: 26 Arrested at Occupy Foreclosure Auction Blockade January 27, 2012, *In These Times.*

vision has already impacted city council proposals, debates and resolutions, such as the case of New York City Council Resolution 1172, which formally opposes corporate personhood and calls for an amendment to the U.S. Constitution to permanently ban it. The resolution creates clear dividing lines between the rights of corporations and the rights of citizens, and it adds to the momentum produced by a growing list of cities—including Los Angeles, Oakland, Albany and Boulder— that have passed similar resolutions.*

Underling Occupy's success has been its focus on the daily details of organizing. Major protests, civil disobedience and arrests are key parts of movement strategy, but the day-to-day activities of discussion, working groups and general assemblies are the deep structure, the ongoing forces adding mass and momentum to Occupy's wave. The locales number in the hundreds, perhaps thousands. In New York City there's Occupy Wall Street, but there's also Occupy Brooklyn, Occupy Sunset Park, Occupy the Bronx, Occupy Long Island, Occupy the Hood and campus organizing like Occupy Columbia University. And online technology, like that used to create InterOccupy.

---

* Bailey McCann, "Cities, states pass resolutions against corporate personhood," January 4, 2012, CivSource. http://civsource-online.com/2012/01/04/cities-states-pass-resolutions-against-corporate-personhood/

org, is connecting Occupy forces around the country and helping to facilitate regional gatherings, strategies and actions.

What makes this all the more remarkable is that despite the "inevitable repression," as Chomsky calls it—the pushback of police brutality, mass arrests, trumped-up charges, restrictive city ordinances, surveillance, infiltration and raids—the movement continues to grow, occupying new fronts from inner-city neighborhoods and local courtrooms to the halls of Congress. Simply continuing in the face of repression can be considered an achievement. With a presence in hundreds of cities, mounting numbers of arrests and big plans for more actions up to the presidential elections and beyond, the movement is also very much occupying the court system and challenging the political nature of government repression.

The movement's tenacity and growth demonstrate the degree to which huge numbers of people no longer believe the system listens or responds to ordinary people. The economic recession is linked to a recession of democracy. The latter is a recession so profound that many politicians no longer hide the fact that they do not listen. During a Republican presidential debate moderated by CNN anchor Anderson Cooper, for example, one of the candidates was asked an immigration-related question. When he ignored the question and rambled on about something else, Cooper pushed him to answer. Dismissing Cooper, the politician snarled, "You get to ask the questions, I get to answer like I want to," drawing loud boos from the live audience.[*]

But booing isn't enough. Politicians' open abandonment of the public interest, accountability and commitment to real democracy is precisely what has driven people from all walks of life to camp out in wind, snow and rain and face tear gas, pepper spray, stun grenades, handcuffs and jail time. People are waking up and coming out. They are blocking bridges and shutting down ports. They are marching in the streets, forming affinity groups, creating their own media, finally speaking up, finally being heard. Protest and civil disobedience are now just the ever-changing surface of something deeper and more powerful: an evolving public insurgency with openness, democracy and non-violent direct action as its primary weapons. That's what's been happening since September 2011, and that's what is happening right now.

In no rush to produce leaders or to issue a closed set of demands, Occupy embodies a vision

---

[*] Emily Ramshaw and Jay Root, "A New Rick Perry Shows Up to GOP Debate," *The Texas Tribune*, October 18, 2011.

of democracy that is fundamentally antagonistic to the management of society as a corporate-controlled space that funds a political system to serve the wealthy, ignore the poor and answer everyone else the same way the politician answered Anderson Cooper: however the hell it wants.

Instead of "letting the market solve things" the way it solved things for the elderly couple in Maine, people are demanding new sorts of solutions, and demanding of themselves the diligence and creativity to invent them. The emerging shift in consciousness is profound, but it's only a step toward further, fuller transformation. People are waking up to the fact that we won't get the necessary change from someone else, from somewhere else, from corporate-financed politicians or simply by voting. The Obama presidency may have been better than that of Bush, but it has not delivered what millions of voting Americans, myself included, wanted and continue to want—a liberating "change we can believe in."

Perhaps the movement's most radical message is its incitement to change ourselves, individually, in the workplace and socially. Chomsky touches on this when he discusses the importance of redefining ideas like growth. If we continue to pursue the dominant model, he says, we'll be like "lemmings walking over a cliff." Instead, he encourages the movement to continue spreading ideas about "a different way of living" that is based not on maximizing how much we can buy, but on "maximizing values that are important for life." Expecting elected officials to turn things around on their own is to go the way of the lemming. No one is going to do it for us. As the black feminist poet June Jordan said, "We are the ones we have been waiting for."

Occupy advocates democracy as the best way to work things out, and conducts its advocacy by example. In the words of the New York Occupy, "Through consensual, non-hierarchical, and participatory self-governance, we are literally laying the framework for a new world by building it here and now—and it works." In practice it's hard work, and debates rage as to what forms of democracy, participation and representation are least prone to corruption and corporate influence.

Challenging corporate manipulation of the economy reveals connected forms of cultural domination and social control, and the process leads to deeper questioning. "How can we find ways to work together to overcome barriers and tensions and become part of a dedicated, ongoing, sustained movement which is going to last a long time?" asks Chomsky. "How can we be together in a unity that is complex and emancipatory?" asks Angela Davis. *How can we get it together?*

In the spirit of asking and exploring answers to those questions—in general assemblies, in protests, in civil disobedience, in print, over the airwaves, in the streets, across borders, in many languages, in jail, in courts and in the freedom of Occupied spaces—the Open Magazine Pamphlet Series, founded in 1991 to give voice to democracy movements, is partnering with the Brooklyn-based immigrant advocacy group Adelante Alliance to launch Zuccotti Park Press and the Occupied Media Pamphlet Series. This is pamphlet #1: a series of talks and conversations with Noam Chomsky about the movement that opens and closes by remembering Howard Zinn.

Although it's winter in New York, our intent is for these little publications to act as seeds of the insurgent imagination, helping to sprout a beautiful American Spring. As Zinn wrote, "Where progress has been made, wherever any kind of injustice has been overturned, it's been because people acted as citizens, and not as politicians. They didn't just moan. They worked, they acted, they organized, they rioted if necessary to bring their situation to the attention of people in power. And that's what we have to do today. Some people might say, 'Well, what do you expect?'

"And the answer is that we expect a lot.

"People say, 'What, are you a dreamer?'

"And the answer is yes, we're dreamers.

"We want it all."

It is in that spirit, in Howard's Zinn's beautiful spirit, that we invite you to join us in launching this new project.

May 10 million flowers bloom.

—Greg Ruggiero
March 12, 2012

OCCUPY YOUR HEART

ANOTHER WORLD
IS POSSIBLE,

Make READY your
DREAMS

I Still
Can't EAT GNP
but I can SEE
CLIMATE
CHANGE
AT MY WINDOW

Noam Chomsky addressing Occupy Boston in
Dewey Square, October 22, 2011.

OCCUPY
Howard Zinn Memorial Lecture

Occupy Boston, MA, Dewey Square, October 22, 2011

It's a little hard to give a Howard Zinn memorial lecture at an Occupy meeting. There are mixed feelings, necessarily, that go along with it. First of all, there's regret that Howard is not here to take part in and invigorate it in his inimitable way, something that would have been the dream of his life. Secondly, there is excitement that the dream is actually being fulfilled. It's a dream for which he laid a lot of the groundwork, and it would have been the fulfillment of a dream for him to have been here with you.

Whenever I think about Howard, which is quite often, particularly in light of the Occupy movement, there are words of his that always resonate in my mind. They are his call to focus our attention on "the countless small actions of unknown people" that are the foundation for "those great moments" that ultimately enter the historical record without the countless small actions of unknown people that created them. That's a fundamental truth of history. And it's one that his work, and in fact his life, did a great deal to illuminate.

It's no exaggeration to say that he literally changed the consciousness and also the conscience of an entire generation. It's no small achievement. And it continues and expands.

A Howard Zinn memorial lecture could not have been better timed. It's taking place in the midst of "countless small actions of unknown people" who are rising.

The Occupy movement is an extremely exciting development. In fact, it's kind of spectacular. It's unprecedented. There's never been anything like it that I can think of.

If the bonds and associations that are being established in these remarkable events can be sustained through a long, hard period ahead—because victory won't come quickly—it could turn out to be a really historic, and very significant, moment in American history.

The fact that the Occupy movement is unprecedented is quite appropriate. It's an unprecedented era. Not just this moment, but since the 1970s.

On the History of the U.S. Economy

The 1970s began a major turning point in American history. For centuries, since the country began, it had been a developing society, and not always in very pretty ways. That's another story, but it was a developing society, with ups and downs. But the general progress was towards wealth, industrialization, development, and hope. There was a pretty constant expectation that it was going to go on like this. That was true even in very dark times.

I'm just old enough to remember the Great Depression. After the first few years, by the mid-1930s—although the situation was objectively much harsher than it is today—nevertheless, the spirit was quite different. There was a sense that "we're gonna get out of it," even among unemployed people, including a lot of my relatives, a sense that "it will get better."

There was militant labor union organizing, especially CIO (Congress of Industrial Organizations), organizing going on. It was getting to the point of sit-down strikes, which are really very frightening to the business world—you could see it in the business press at the time—because a sit-down strike is just a step before taking over the factory and running it yourself. The idea of worker takeovers is something which is, incidentally, very much on the agenda today, and we should keep it in mind—I'll come back to it. Also the New Deal legislations were beginning to come in as a result of popular pressure. Despite the hard times, there was a sense that, somehow, "we're gonna get out of it."

It's quite different now. For many people in the United States, there's kind of a pervasive sense of hopelessness, sometimes despair. I think it's quite new in American history. And it has an objective basis.

On the Working Class

In the 1930s, unemployed working people could anticipate that their jobs would come back. If you're a worker in manufacturing today (the current level of unemployment in manufacturing is approximately like the Depression) and current tendencies persist, those jobs aren't going to come back.

The change took place in the 1970s. There are a lot of reasons for it. One of the underlying factors, discussed mainly by economic historian Robert Brenner, was the falling rate of profit in manufacturing. There were other factors. It led to major changes in the economy—a reversal of the several hundred years of progress towards industrialization and development and that turned to a process of de-industrialization and de-development. Of course, manufacturing production continued overseas—very profitable, but no good for the work force.

Along with that came a significant shift of the economy from productive enterprise—producing

things people need or could use—to financial manipulation. The financialization of the
economy really took off at that time.

On Banks

Before the 1970s, banks were banks. They did
what banks were supposed to do in a state capi-
talist economy: they took unused funds from your
bank account, for example, and transferred them
to some potentially useful purpose like helping
some family to buy a home or send a kid to college,
or whatever it might be. That changed dramatically
in the 1970s. Until then, there were no financial
crises. It was a period of enormous growth—the
highest growth in American history, maybe in
economic history—sustained growth through the
1950s and 1960s. And it was egalitarian.

So the lowest quintile did about as well as the
highest quintile. Lots of people moved into rea-
sonable lifestyles. What's called here "middle
class." "Working class," as it's called in other
countries. But it was real.

And the 1960s accelerated it. The activism of
the 1960s, after a pretty dismal decade, really civilized the country in lots of ways that are permanent. They're not changing. They're staying on.

When the 1970s came along there were sudden
and sharp changes: de-industrialization, off-

shoring of production, and shifting to financial institutions, which grew enormously. I should say that, in the 1950s and 1960s, there was also the development of what several decades later became the high-tech economy: computers, the Internet, the IT Revolution, mostly developed in the 1950s and 1960s, substantially in the state sector. It took a couple of decades before it took off, but it was developed there.

The developments that took place during the 1970s set off a vicious cycle. It led to concentration of wealth increasingly in the hands of the financial sector. This doesn't benefit the economy—it probably harms it and the society—but it did lead to tremendous concentration of wealth, substantially there.

On Politics and Money

Concentration of wealth yields concentration of political power. And concentration of political power gives rise to legislation that increases and accelerates the cycle. The legislation, essentially bipartisan, drives new fiscal policies, tax changes, also rules of corporate governance, and deregulation. Alongside of this began the very sharp rise in the costs of elections, which drives the political parties even deeper than before into the pockets of the corporate sector.

The parties dissolved, essentially, in many ways. It used to be that if a person in Congress hoped for a position such as a committee chair or some position of responsibility, he or she got it mainly through seniority and service. Within a couple of years, they started having to put money into the party coffers in order to get ahead, a topic studied mainly by Tom Ferguson. That just drove the whole system even deeper into the pockets of the corporate sector, increasingly the financial sector.

This cycle resulted in a tremendous concentration of wealth, mainly in the top tenth of one percent of the population. Meanwhile, for the general population, it began to open a period of stagnation or even decline for the majority. People got by, but by artificial means such as longer working hours, high rates of borrowing and debt, and reliance on asset inflation like the recent housing bubble. Pretty soon those working hours were much higher in the United States than in other industrial countries like Japan and those in Europe. So there was a period of stagnation and decline for the majority that continued alongside a period of sharp concentration of wealth. The political system began to dissolve.

There has always been a gap between public policy and public will, but it just grew astronomically. You can see it right now, in fact.

Take a look at what's happening right now.

The big topic in Washington that everyone concentrates on is the deficit. For the public, correctly, the deficit is not regarded as much of an issue. And it isn't really much of an issue. The issue is joblessness, not the deficit. There's a deficit commission but there's no joblessness commission. As far as the deficit is concerned, the public has opinions. Take a look at the polls. The public overwhelmingly supports higher taxes on the wealthy, which have declined sharply in this period of stagnation and decline—higher taxes on the wealthy and preserve the limited social benefits.

The outcome of the deficit commission is probably going to be the opposite. Either they'll reach an agreement, which will be the opposite of what the public wants, or else it will go into a kind of automatic procedure that is going to have those effects. Actually, that's something that has to be dealt with very quickly.

The deficit commission is going to come up with its decision in a couple of weeks. The Occupy movements could provide a mass base for trying to avert what amounts to a dagger pointed at the heart of the country. It could have very negative effects. It's an immediate task.

On Economics

Without going into details, what's been playing out for the past thirty years is actually a nightmare that was anticipated by the classical economists.

Adam Smith considered the possibility that merchants and manufacturers in England might decide to do their business abroad—invest abroad and import from abroad. He said they would profit, but England would be harmed.

However, he went on to say that the merchants and manufacturers would prefer to operate in their own country—what's sometimes called a "home bias." So, as if by "an invisible hand," England would be saved from the ravages of what is now called neoliberal globalization. That's a pretty hard passage to miss. In his classic *Wealth of Nations*, that's the only occurrence of the phrase, "invisible hand." Maybe England would be saved from neoliberal globalization by an "invisible hand."

The other great classical economist, David Ricardo, recognized the same thing and hoped that it wouldn't happen—kind of a sentimental hope—and it didn't for a long time. But now it is happening. Over the last thirty years that's exactly what has been underway.

Plutonomy and the Precariat

For the general population, the 99 percent in the imagery of the Occupy movement, it's been pretty harsh. And it could get worse. This could be a period of irreversible decline. For the 1 percent and even less—the one-tenth of the 1 percent— it's just fine. They are richer than ever, more powerful than ever, controlling the political system, disregarding the public. And if it can continue, as far as they're concerned, sure, why not? Just what Adam Smith and David Ricardo warned about.

Take, for example, Citigroup. For decades, Citigroup has been one of the most corrupt of the major investment banking corporations, repeatedly bailed out by the taxpayer, starting in the early Reagan years and now once again. I won't run through the corruption—you probably already know about it—but it's pretty astonishing.

In 2005, Citigroup came out with a brochure for investors called "Plutonomy: Buying Luxury, Explaining Global Imbalances." The brochure urged investors to put money into a "plutonomy index." The memo says "the World is dividing into two blocs - the Plutonomy and the rest."

Plutonomy refers to the rich, those who buy luxury goods and so on, and that's where the action is. They said that their plutonomy index was way out-performing the stock market, so people should put money into it. As for the rest, we send 'em adrift. We don't really care about them. We don't really need 'em. They have to be around to provide a powerful state, which will protect us and bail us out when we get into trouble, but other than that they essentially have no function. These days they're sometimes called the "precariat"—people who live a precarious existence at the periphery of society. It's not the periphery anymore. It's becoming a very substantial part of the society in the United States, and indeed elsewhere. And this is considered a good thing.

So, for example, Alan Greenspan, at the time when he was still "Saint Alan"—hailed by the economics profession as one of the greatest economists of all time (this was before the crash for which he was substantially responsible)—was testifying to Congress in the Clinton years, and he explained the wonders of the great economy that he was supervising. He said a lot of the success of this economy was based substantially on what he called "growing worker insecurity." If working people are insecure, if they're part of what we now call the "precariat," living precarious existences, they're not going to make demands, they're not going to try to get wages, they won't get benefits. We can kick 'em out if we don't need 'em. And that's what's called a "healthy" economy, technically. And he was very highly praised for this, greatly admired.

Well, now the world is indeed splitting into a plutonomy and a precariat—again, in the imagery of the Occupy movement, the 1 percent and the 99 percent. Not literal numbers, but the right picture. Now, the plutonomy is where the action is. Well, it could continue like this.

If it does continue like this, the historic reversal that began in the 1970s could become irreversible. That's where we're heading. And the Occupy movement is the first real, major popular reaction that could avert this. But, as I said, it's going to be necessary to face the fact that it's a long, hard struggle. You don't win victories tomorrow. You have to go on, have to form the structures that will be sustained, that will go on through hard times and can win major victories. And there are a lot of things that can be done.

Toward Worker Takeover

I mentioned before that, in the 1930s, one of the most effective actions was the sit-down strike. And the reason is very simple: that's just a step before takeover of the industry.

Through the 1970s, as the decline was setting in, there were some very important events that took place. One was in the late '70s. In 1977, U.S.

Steel decided to close one of its major facilities in Youngstown, Ohio. Instead of just walking away, the workforce and the community decided to get together and buy it from U.S. Steel, hand it over to the work force, and turn it into a worker-run, worker-managed facility. They didn't win. But, with enough popular support, they could have won. It was a partial victory. It's a topic that Gar Alperovitz and Staughton Lynd—the lawyer for the workers and community—have discussed in detail.

It was a partial victory because, even though they lost, it set off other efforts. And now, throughout Ohio, and in fact in other places, there's a scattering of hundreds, maybe thousands, of sometimes not-so-small worker/community-owned industries that could become worker-managed. And that's the basis for a real revolution. That's how it takes place. It's happening here, too.

In one of the suburbs of Boston, about a year ago, something similar happened. A multinational decided to close down a profitable, functioning manufacturing facility carrying out some high-tech manufacturing. Evidently, it just wasn't profitable enough for them. The workforce and the union offered to buy it, take it over, and run it themselves. The multinational decided to close it down instead, probably for reasons of class-consciousness. I don't think they want things like this to happen. If there had been enough popular support, if there had been something like this movement that could have gotten involved, they might have succeeded.

And there are other things going on like that. In fact, some of them are major. Not long ago, Obama took over the auto industry, which was basically owned by the public. And there were a number of things that could have been done. One was what was done: reconstitute it so that it can be handed back to the ownership, or very similar ownership, and continue on its traditional path.

The other possibility was to hand it over to the workforce—which owned it anyway—turn it into a worker-owned, worker-managed major industrial system that's a big part of the economy, and have it produce things that people need. And there's a lot that we need.

We all know or should know that the United States is extremely backward globally in high-speed transportation, and it's very serious. It not only affects people's lives, but it affects the economy.

In that regard, here's a personal story. I happened to be giving talks in France a couple of months ago and ended up in Southern France and had to take a train from Avignon to Charles De Gaulle Airport in Paris. It took two hours. The trip we took was the same distance as from Washington, DC, to Boston. I don't know if you've ever taken the train from Washington to Boston, but it's operating at about the same speed it was sixty years ago when my wife and I first took it. It's a scandal. It could be done here as it's been done in Europe. They had the capacity to do it, the skilled work force. It would have taken a little popular support, but it could have made a major change in the economy.

Just to make it more surreal, while this option was being avoided, the Obama administration was sending its transportation secretary to Spain to get contracts for developing high-speed rail for the United States, which could have been done right in the rust belt, which is being closed down. There are no economic reasons why this can't happen. These are class reasons, and reflect the lack of popular political mobilization. Things like this continue.

Climate Change and Nuclear Weapons

Let me just say that I've kept to domestic issues, and these are by no means the only ones. You all know that. There are very dangerous developments in the international arena, including two of them, which are a kind of a shadow that hangs over everything we've discussed. There are, for the first time in human history, real threats to decent survival of the species.

Two are particularly urgent. One has been hanging around since 1945. It's kind of a miracle that we've escaped it. That's the threat of nuclear war and nuclear weapons. Though it isn't being much discussed, that threat is in fact being escalated by policies of this administration and its allies. And something has to be done about that or we're in real trouble.

The other, of course, is environmental catastrophe. Practically every country in the world is taking at least halting steps towards trying to do something about it. The United States is also taking steps, mainly to accelerate the threat.

The United States is the only major country that is not only not doing something constructive to protect the environment. It's not climbing on the train. In some ways it's pulling it backwards.

Congress right now is dismantling legislation instituted by Richard Nixon—really the last liberal president of the U.S., literally, and that shows you what's been going on. They're dismantling the limited measures of the Nixon administration to try to do something about what is a growing, emerging catastrophe.

And this is connected with a huge propaganda system, proudly and openly declared by the business world, to try to convince people that climate change is just a liberal hoax. "Why pay attention to these scientists?" And we're really regressing back to the medieval period. It's not a joke.

If that's happening in the most powerful, richest country in history, then this catastrophe isn't going to be averted. And everything else we're talking about won't matter in a generation or two. All that is going on right now. Something has to be done about it very soon, in a dedicated, sustained way.

It's not going to be easy to proceed. There are going to be barriers, difficulties, hardships, failures—it's inevitable. But unless the process that is taking place here and elsewhere in the country and around the world, unless that continues to grow and to become a major force in the social and political world, the chances for a decent future are not very high.

QUESTIONS FROM OCCUPY BOSTON

Regarding fixing political dysfunction in this country, what about enacting a Constitutional amendment to abolish corporate personhood or to get corporate money out of politics?

These would be very good things to do, but you can't do this or anything else unless there is a large, active, popular base. If the Occupy movement was the leading force in the country, you could push many things forward.

But remember, most people don't know that this is happening. Or they may know it is happening, but don't know what it is. And among those who do know, polls show that there's a lot of support.

That assigns a task. It's necessary to get out into the country and get people to understand what this is about, and what they can do about it, and what the consequences are of not doing anything about it.

Corporate personhood is an important case in point, but pay attention to what it is. We should think about it. We're supposed to worship the U.S. Constitution these days. The Fifth Amendment says that "no person shall be deprived" of rights "without due process of law." Well, by "person," the Founding Fathers didn't actually mean "person." So, for example, there were a lot of creatures of flesh and blood that weren't considered to be "persons." The indigenous population, for example. They didn't have any rights. In the U.S. Constitution there was a category of creatures called three-fifth humans—the enslaved population. They weren't considered persons. And in fact women were barely considered persons, so they didn't have rights.

A lot of this was somewhat rectified over the years. After the Civil War, the Fourteenth Amendment raised the three-fifths humans to full humans, at least in principle. But that was only in principle. Soon other methods were instituted to criminalize Black life, which led to virtual restoration of a kind of slavery. In fact, something like that is happening again now, as the processes of neoliberal globalization I was talking about leave a superfluous population among the precariat; and with the fairly close class-race-ethnicity relation in the United States, that means largely Black, secondarily Hispanic.

Over the following years, the concept of "person" was changed by the courts in two ways. One way was to broaden it to include corporations, legal fictions established and sustained by the state. In fact, these "persons" later became the management of corporations, according to the court decisions. So the management of corporations became "persons."

It was also narrowed to exclude undocumented immigrants. They had to be excluded from the category of "persons." And that's happening right now. So the legislations that you're talking about, they go two ways. They broaden the category of persons to include corporate entities, which now have rights way beyond human beings, given by the trade agreements and others, and they exclude the people who flee from Central America where the U.S. devastated their homelands, and flee from Mexico because they can't compete with the highly-subsidized U.S. agribusiness.

Remember that, when NAFTA was passed in 1994, the Clinton administration understood pretty well that it was going to devastate the Mexican economy, and that's the year when they started militarizing the border. Well, now we're getting the consequences, and these people have to be excluded from the category of persons. So when you talk about personhood—that's right—but there's more than one aspect to it, and it ought to be pushed forward and all of it understood and acted upon.

That requires a mass base. It requires that the population understands this and is committed to it. It's easy to think of things that need to be done, but they all have a prerequisite, namely, a mass popular base that is committed to implementing it.

How likely is it that the ruling class in America could develop an openly fascist system here?

I think it's very unlikely, frankly. They don't have the force. About a century ago, in the freest countries in the world at that time—Britain and the United States—the dominant classes came to understand that they can't control the population by force any longer. Too much freedom had been won by struggles like these. They realized this, they were self-conscious about it, and it's discussed in their literature.

The dominant class recognized they had to shift their tactics to control of attitudes and beliefs instead of just the cudgel. They didn't throw away the cudgel, but it can't do what it used to do. You have to control attitudes and beliefs. In fact, that's when the public relations industry began. It began in the United States and England, the free countries where you had to have a major industry to control beliefs and attitudes; to induce consumerism, passivity, apathy, distraction—all the things you know very well. And that's the way it's been going on. It's a barrier, but it's a lot easier to overcome than torture and the Gestapo. I don't think the circumstances exist any longer for instituting anything like what we called fascism.

Sir, I have a two-part question that I've been waiting to ask you my whole life. You mentioned earlier that sit-down protests are just a precursor to a takeover of industry. I'd like to ask you if, today, you would advocate a general strike as an effective tactic for moving forward; and second, would you ever, if asked, allow for your voice to relay the democratically chosen will of our nation?

My voice wouldn't help. And besides, you don't want leaders; you want to do it yourselves. [Applause and cheers] We need representation, but you need to pick them yourselves and they need to be recallable representatives. We're not going to fall into some system of control and hierarchy.

But the question of the general strike is like the others. You can think of it as a possible idea at a time when the population is ready for it. We can't sit here and just declare a general strike. Obviously, there has to be approval, agreement, and willingness to take the risks to participate on the part of the large mass of the population. There has to be organization, education, activism. Education doesn't mean just telling people what to believe. It means learning things for ourselves.

There is a famous line by Karl Marx, which I am sure many of you know: the task is not just to understand the world, but to change it. And there is a variant of that which should also be kept in mind. If you want to change the world in a constructive direction, you better try to understand it first. And understanding it doesn't mean just listening to a talk or reading a book, although that's helpful sometimes. It means learning. And you learn through participation. You learn from others. You learn from the people you are trying to organize. And you have to gain the experience and understanding which will make it possible to maybe implement ideas like that as a tactic.

But there is a long way to go, and you don't get there by a flick of the wrist. That happens by hard, long-term, dedicated work.

And I think that maybe, in many ways, the most exciting aspect of the Occupy movement is the construction of the associations, bonds, linkages and networks that are taking place all over—whether it's a collaborative kitchen or something else. And, out of that, if it can be sustained and expanded to a large part of the population who doesn't yet know what is going on. If that can happen, then you can raise questions about tactics like a general strike that could very well at some point be appropriate.

We have two questions about Occupy worldwide: First, how do you think we can effectively target problems to bring about change? And should we make demands?

They should have proposals and ideas, and there doesn't have to be agreement on them. There's good reason to "let a hundred flowers bloom." There are lots of possibilities, but there are very sensible proposals, starting from very short-term ones. Let's prevent the deficit commission from carrying out a very lethal blow against society that might have lasting effects in the next couple of weeks. That's pretty short-term.

There are longer-terms things, like the ones I mentioned—helping the workforce in the Boston suburb I mentioned to take over their own industry, instead of becoming jobless. Then going on to maybe do the same thing with the whole manufacturing industry. And there are many things like that coming along.

Turning the country into a leader in the effort to try to mitigate—maybe overcome—the tremendous threat of global warming, instead of being a follower in that regard, or in fact a leader, and practically the only participant, in the campaign to accelerate the threat.

All of those are things that you can do. We should have those proposals. Dealing with corporate personhood is another proposal, but I would suggest that it be broadened to deal with the distortion—the gross distortion—in the concept of person, which both broadens it to include corporate entities and narrows it to exclude legally defined non-people. And there are plenty of other demands I could think of. They should be formulated. Not everyone has to agree on the ranking of priorities or even the choice of demands, but groups can pursue them. There is a lot that can be done.

Should we rewrite the system? How can we mobilize the American public?

The only way to mobilize the American public that I've ever heard of—or any other public— is by going out and joining them. Going out to wherever people are—churches, clubs, schools, unions—wherever they may be. Getting involved with them and trying to learn from them and to bring about a change of consciousness among them. And, again, this can be very concrete.

Let's take the electoral system in the United States. It has a lot of flaws—like what I mentioned: public policy and public opinion are so radically divorced. But there are some narrower things that you can do something about right away.

We're coming up to the presidential election's primary season. Suppose we had a functioning democratic society. Let's just imagine that. What would a primary look like, say, in New Hampshire? What would happen in a primary would be that the people in a town would get together and discuss, talk about, and argue about what they want policy to be. Sort of like what's been happening here in the Occupy movement. They should formulate a conception of what the policy should be. Then if a candidate comes along and says, "I want to come talk to you," the people in the town ought to say, "Well, you can come listen to us if you want. So you come in, we'll tell you what we want, and you can try to persuade us that you'll do it; then, maybe we will vote for you." That's what would happen in a democratic society.

What happens in our society? The candidate comes to town with his public relations agents and the rest of them. He gives some talks, and says,

"Look how great I am. This is what I am going to do for you." Anybody with a grey-cell functioning doesn't believe a word he or she says. And then maybe people vote for him, maybe they don't. That's very different from a democratic society.

Making moves in the direction of real democracy is not utopian. Those are things that can be done in particular communities. And it could lead to a noticeable change in the political system.

Sure, we should get money out of politics, but that's going to take a lot of work. One way to go at it is just to elect your own representatives. It's not impossible. The same is true all across the board.

Let's go back to the deficit again. The population understands that it's not the primary problem. In fact, it's not even a major problem. The population has a sensible attitude about what ought to be done with it, like higher taxes for the rich and going back to the way things were during the big growth periods and preserving the benefits—they're limited, and they ought to be improved.

And there's something else that isn't even being discussed. The deficit would be eliminated, literally, if the United States had a health care system of a kind that other industrial countries have. [Loud applause] You know, that's literally true. It's not utopian. The idea that we should have health care like other industrial countries is not wild radical raving. [Laughter]

The health care system in the United States, I'm sure you know, is a total international scandal. It's twice the per capita cost of comparable countries and one of the worst outcomes, with a huge number of people uninsured altogether. And it's going to get worse.

The problem is not Medicare. Medicare is indeed a problem, but it's a problem because it goes through the privatized, largely unregulated system that is totally dysfunctional.

You can't talk about this in Washington because of the power of financial institutions. A large part of the public wants it. In fact, for decades substantial parts of the population, often big majorities, have been in favor of this, but it can't be talked about. There's too much power now in the financial institutions. But that can be changed. It's not pie in the sky. And to the extent that the deficit is a problem, that's one thing that can be done about it.

The other thing that can be done, you all know about: reining in our crazed military system, which has about the same expenses as the militaries of the rest of the world combined. But our military system is not for defense. In fact, it's actually harmful to us, if you look at it. It doesn't have to be like that.

So there are things that are quite feasible. Proposals have to be made and brought to the population in a convincing way. And most of the population already agrees with most these things. But you have to turn the population into a force that will be active and engaged. Then you could have results.

Professor Chomsky, what are your thoughts on publicly financed campaigns?

Occupy Facilitator: I also have two points of information. This presentation is on the live stream and will be recorded and posted to occupyboston.org.

Another point of information is that there is now "Occupy Congress." Look for it on the Web. It's very new. Let's just do it!

Well, I think that's a pretty good answer to the question about what we should do about publicly financed campaigns: Let's just do it. We pick our own representatives. We finance them. We vote for them. If the corporations pour money into somebody else's pockets, they can spend it on luxury goods. That can be done, but only if you have an organized and engaged public.

There are lots of things you can propose. They all go back to the same basic conclusion: You have to have an organized, dedicated public that is willing to implement them. If there is, a lot of options open up, including these.

Could you please share your thoughts on the significance of the Occupy the 'Hood movement, and any insights you may have regarding cross-cultural organization for social change?

That's a great movement. I heard, just coming out here this evening, that the first Occupy the 'Hood action took place just yesterday in Boston. And it's been happening in other places, New York, and elsewhere.

That's perfect. It's just the kind of reaching out in the general community that makes sense. People have to do it themselves. I can't tell people at an Occupy in Roxbury what to do, and if I did, they shouldn't listen to me. They know how to do it.

We should work hard to get this integrated. And that means again, not just telling people "here's what you should believe," but learning from them. What do they want? What do they need? What can we learn from them? How can we find ways to work together to overcome barriers and tensions and become part of a dedicated, ongoing, sustained movement which is going to last a long time?

Most of these goals that we are talking about cannot be attained in a couple of weeks or months—actually some of them can—but most of them involve a long struggle.

People with power don't give it up unless they have to. And that takes work.

AFTER THIRTY YEARS OF CLASS WAR

Interview with Edward Radzivilovskiy, Student, New York University, Paris

Interview conducted at MIT, Cambridge, Massachusetts, January 6, 2012

I want to start off with something you said at Occupy Boston: "The most exciting aspect of the Occupy movement is the construction of the linkages that are taking place all over. If they can be sustained and expanded, Occupy can lead to dedicated efforts to set society on a more humane course."*

Some have said that the Occupy movement does not have a cohesive message of its demands. If you do believe that the Occupy movement does have specific demands, how many of these demands do you actually think can be realized?

There is quite a range of people from many walks of life and many concerns involved in the Occupy

---

* Noam Chomsky, "Occupy the Future," *inthesetimes.com*, November 1, 2011, http://www.inthesetimes.com/article/12206/occupy_the_future/.

movement. There are some general things that bring them together, but of course they all have specific concerns as well.

Primarily, I think this should be regarded as a response, the first major public response, in fact, to about thirty years of a really quite bitter class war that has led to social, economic and political arrangements in which the system of democracy has been shredded.

Congress, for example, has its lowest approval level in history—practically invisible—and other institutions' ratings are not much higher.

The population is angry, frustrated, bitter—and for good reasons. For the past generation, policies have been initiated that have led to an extremely sharp concentration of wealth in a tiny sector of the population. In fact, the wealth distribution is very heavily weighted by, literally, the top tenth of one percent of the population, a fraction so small that they're not even picked up on the census. You have to do statistical analysis just to detect them. And they have benefited enormously. This is mostly from the financial sector—hedge fund managers, CEOs of financial corporations, and so on.

At the same time, for the majority of the population, incomes have pretty much stagnated. Real wages have also stagnated, sometimes declined. The benefits system that was very strong has been weakened.

People have been getting by in the United States by much higher workloads, by debt which sooner or later becomes unsustainable, and by the illusions created by bubbles—most recently, the housing bubble which collapsed, like bubbles do, leaving about $8 trillion in paper wealth disappearing for some sectors of the population. So, by now, U.S. workers put in far more hours than their counterparts in other industrial countries, and for African Americans almost all wealth has disappeared. It has been a pretty harsh and bitter period—not by the standards of developing nations, but this is a rich society and people judge their situation and their prospects by what *ought* to be the case.

At the same time, concentration of wealth leads almost reflexively to concentration of political power, which in turn translates into legislation, naturally in the interests of those implementing it; and that accelerates what has been a vicious cycle leading to, as I said, bitterness, anger, frustration and a very atomized society. That's why the linkages in the Occupy movement are so important.

Occupy is really the first sustained response to this. People have referred to the Tea Party as a response, but that is highly misleading. The Tea Party is relatively affluent, white. Its influence and power come from the fact that it has enormous corporate support and heavy finance. Parts of the corporate world simply see them as their shock troops, but it's not a movement in the serious sense that Occupy is.

Going back to your question about the movement's demands, there are general ones that are very widely shared in the population: Concern about the inequality. Concern about the chicanery of the financial institutions and the way their influence on the government has led to a situation in which those responsible for the crisis are helped out, bailed out—richer and more powerful than ever, while the victims are ignored. There are very specific proposals concerning the regulation of financial transaction taxes, reversal of the rules of corporate governance that have led to this kind of situation: for example, a shifting of the tax code back to something more like what it used to be when the very rich were not essentially exempted from taxes, and many other quite specific demands of that kind. It goes on to include the interests of groups and their particular concerns, some of which are quite far reaching.

But I think, if you investigate the Occupy movements and you ask them what are their demands, they are reticent to answer and rightly so, because they are essentially crafting a point of view from many disparate sources. And one of the striking features of the movement has simply been the creation of cooperative communities—something very much lacking in an atomized, disintegrated society—that include general assemblies that carry out extensive discussion, kitchens, libraries, support systems, and so on. All of that is a work in progress leading to community structures that, if they can spread out into the broader community and retain their vitality, could be very important.

Colin Asher, a journalist, wrote a piece for The Progressive, *in which he says, "Most scribes have settled on the idea that Occupy Wall Street is like Tahrir Square in Egypt, but I disagree. Occupy Wall Street is more like a Hooverville. The space itself engages people's imaginations, but nothing will be settled here, not even the meaning of what is happening, and the participants won't be able to define it. It matters that something is happening in lower Manhattan, and that people are paying attention, but it doesn't much matter what is happening."**

And you have said, "The 2012 election is now expected to cost two billion dollars. It's going to have to be mostly corporate funding. So it's not at all surprising that Obama is selecting business leaders for top positions. The public is quite angry and frus-

---

* Colin Asher, "Occupy Wall St. in NYC—The Week That Was," *The Progressive*, October 16, 2011.

trated, but unless Western populations can rise to the level of Egyptians they're going to remain victims."

So what I am wondering is, do you see the Occupy movement as an anarchist movement—the kind of uprising you have been advocating for most of your career? Is it a precursor to a revolution, or can these goals be achieved without a revolution?

First of all, let's talk about Egypt. What happened in Tahrir Square was extremely important, of historic importance in fact, and it did achieve a goal, namely, eliminating the dictatorship. But it left the regime in power. So yes, that's an important goal and there have been achievements: the press is much freer and the labor activism is much less constrained.

In fact, one striking difference between the Egyptian and Tunisian uprisings and the Occupy movements is that, in the North African case, the labor movement was right at the center of it. And, in fact, there is a very close correlation between such successes as there have been in the Middle East and North Africa and the level of labor militancy there over many years. That's been true in Egypt for years. They're usually crushed, but

---

* Noam Chomsky, "The State-Corporate Complex: A Threat to Freedom and Survival," lecture given at the University of Toronto, April 7, 2011. http://chomsky.info/talks/20110407.htm.

some successes. As soon as the labor movement became integrated into the April 6 movement—the Tahrir Square movement—it became a really significant and powerful force.

That's quite different here. The labor movement has been decimated. Part of the task to be carried out is to revitalize it.

In Tunisia they did succeed in getting rid of a dictator and in running a parliamentary election, now with a moderate Islamist party in control.

In Egypt, as I said, there were gains, but the military-run regime is very much in power. There will be a parliamentary election; there has been already. The groups that are succeeding in the elections are those that have been working for years organizing among the general population—the Muslim Brotherhood and the Salafists.

It's quite a different situation here. There hasn't been that kind of large-scale organizing. The labor movement has been struggling to retain victories that it won a long time ago and that it has been losing.

To have a revolution—a meaningful one—you need a substantial majority of the population who recognize or believe that further reform is not possible within the institutional framework that exists. And there is nothing like that here, not even remotely.

Should we be trying to achieve that? Should we be working up to a revolution or should we be trying to achieve it some other way?

First of all, we are nowhere near the limits of what reform can carry out. People can have the idea of a revolution in the back of their minds if they want. But there are very substantive actions that should be taking place.

I don't exactly know what it means to say, "*Is this just anarchist?*" Anarchist movements are very concerned with achieving specific goals. That's what they have traditionally been and that's what they should be. In this case, as I said, there are very specific short-term goals that have large support: fiscal policy, controlling financial institutions, dealing with environmental problems which are extraordinarily significant, shifting the political systems so that elections are not simply blocked, and so on. All of these are very direct and immediate concerns.

For example, just a couple of days ago, New York City's City Council, probably under the influence of the Occupy movement, passed a resolution, unanimously I think, against corporate personhood. The resolution establishes that "corporations are not entitled to the entirety of protections or 'rights' of natural persons, specifically so that the expenditure of corporate money to influence the electoral process is no longer a form of constitutionally protected speech" and calls on Congress "to begin the process of amending the Constitution."*

Well, that's pretty far reaching. It's a very popular idea in this country, and if it's pursued, it will dismantle a century of judicial decisions that have given corporations and state-created fictitious legal entities extraordinary rights and power. The population doesn't like it and has a right not to like it. Such steps are already being taken in words and could lead to action.

In the longer term, there are many things that can be done. For example, in many parts of the country, particularly Ohio, there's quite a significant spread of worker-owned enterprises. As I mentioned to Occupy Boston, a lot of this derived from a major effort, over thirty years ago, when U.S. Steel wanted to sell off and close one of its major installations. The work force and the community offered to buy it and run it themselves— industrial democracy, essentially. That went to the courts and they lost, although with sufficient support they could have won. But even the failure, like many failures, has spawned other efforts. Now there's a network of worker/community-owned enterprises spreading over the region.

---

* New York City Council, Resolution 1172, January 4, 2012.

Is this reform or revolution? If it extends, it's revolution. It changes the institutional structure of the society. Actually, a lot of it is supported by conservatives. It doesn't break very simply or sharply on what's called, mostly meaninglessly, a right-left spectrum. But these are things that respond to people's needs and concerns. There are cases right near here where similar options were possible. And I think those are directions that should definitely be pursued. A lot of these struggles are invigorated by things like the Occupy movement.

Similarly, going back to Egypt where the situation is quite different, they have very immediate concerns, like the question of what will the power of the military regime be. Will it be replaced by Islamist forces based in the slums and rural areas? What place will secular liberal elements— the ones who actually initiated the Tahrir Square demonstrations—find in this system? These are all very concrete problems that they have to deal with. Here, there are different concrete problems to deal with. There are many similarities.

In both cases, in Egypt and the United States, and in fact much the world, what's happening is a reaction—in my opinion a much-too-delayed reaction—to the neoliberal policies of roughly the last thirty years. They have been implemented in different ways in different countries. But it's generally the case that, to the extent that they have been implemented everywhere, they have been harmful to the general population and beneficial to a very small sector. And that's not accidental.

There is a new small book by the Economic Policy Institute called *Failure by Design: The Story behind America's Broken Economy*. And the phrase, "by design," is accurate. These things don't happen by the laws of nature or by principles of economics, to the extent they exist. They're choices. And they are choices made by the wealthy and powerful elements to create a society that answers to their needs. It's happened, and it's happening in Europe right now.

Take the European Central Bank (ECB). There are many economists, Nobel Laureates and others, and I agree with them, who think that the policies that the ECB is following and pursuing—basically austerity in a period of recession—are guaranteed to make the situation worse. So far, I think that's been the case.

Growth is what is needed in a period of recession, not austerity. Europe has the resources to stimulate growth, but their resources are not being used because of the policies of the Central Bank and others. And one can ask what the purpose of this is. And a rational way to judge purposes is to look at predictable consequences. And one consequence is that these policies undermine the social-democratic structures and the welfare-state structure that have been developed; they undermine the power of labor and create a more inegalitarian society, with greater power in the hands of the corporate sector and the wealthy. So it's class war basically, and that's a kind of "failure by design" as well.

I think a lot of people today, when you mention to them an anarchist society, they get the wrong impression. . . . Would you describe anarchist society as an ultra-radical version of democracy?

First of all, nobody owns the concept of "anarchism." Anarchism has a very broad back. You can find all kinds of things in the anarchist movements. So the question of what an anarchist society can be is almost meaningless. Different people who associate themselves with rough anarchist tendencies have very different conceptions.

But the most developed notions that anarchist activists and thinkers have had in mind are those for a highly organized society—highly structured, highly organized—but organized on the basis of free and voluntary participation. So, for example, what I mentioned about the Ohio network of worker/community-owned enterprises, that's a traditional anarchist vision. Enterprises, not only owned but *managed* by participants in a free association with one another is a big step beyond. It could be at the federal level. It could be at the international level. So yes, it's a highly democratic conception of a structured, organized society with power at the base. It doesn't mean that it doesn't have representatives—it can have, but they should be recallable and under the influence and control of participants.

Who's in favor of a society like that? You can say Adam Smith, for example, who believed—you can question whether his beliefs were accurate, but he *believed*—that market systems and the "invisible hand" of individual choices would lead to egalitarian societies of common participation. You can question the logic of the argument, but the goals are understandable and they go far back. You can find them in the first serious book of politics that was ever written, Aristotle's *Politics*.

When Aristotle evaluated various kinds of systems, he felt that democracy was the least bad of them. But he said democracy wouldn't work unless you could set things up so that they would be relatively egalitarian. He proposed specific measures for Athens that, in our terms, would be welfare-state measures.

There are plenty of roots for these concepts. A lot of them come right out of the Enlightenment. But I don't think anyone has the authority to say *this is what an anarchist society is going to look like.* There are people who think you can sketch it out in great detail, but my own feeling here—I essentially agree with Marx—is that these things have to be worked out by people who are living and functioning in freedom and work out for themselves what kinds of societies and communities are appropriate for them.

The late British philosopher, Martin Hollis, worked extensively on questions of human action, the philosophy of social science and rationality. One of the claims he made was that any anarchist vision of a society rests upon an idea of human nature that is too optimistic. In short, he argued that anarchism is only viable if humans by nature are good. He says that history shows us that humans cannot be trusted to this degree; thus, anarchism is too idealistic. Would you mind responding to this objection very quickly, given your commitment to some of the ideals of anarchism?

It's possible to respond to arguments. It is not possible to respond to opinions. If someone makes an assertion saying, "Here's what I believe," that's fine—he can say what he believes, but you can't respond to it. You can ask, what is the basis for your belief? Or, can you provide me with some evidence? What do you know about human nature?

Actually, we don't know very much about human nature. So yes, that's an expression of his belief, and he's entitled to make it. We have no idea, nor does he have any idea, if it's true or false. But it really doesn't matter; whatever the truth turns out to be, we will follow the same policies, namely, trying to optimize and maximize freedom, justice, participation, democracy. Those are goals that we'll attempt to realize. Maybe human beings are such that there's a limit to how far they can be realized; okay, we'll still follow the same policies. So, whatever one's un-argued assertions may be, it has very little effect on the policy and choices.

Professor Chomsky, thank you very much.

INTEROCCUPY

InterOccupy conference call with Noam Chomsky,
Mikal Kamil and Ian Escuela, and questions submitted in
advance by others involved with Occupy, January 31, 2012.
InterOccupy.org provides channels of communications between general
assemblies, working groups and supporters across the Occupy movement.

Professor Chomsky, the Occupy movement is in its second phase. Three of our main goals are to: 1) occupy the mainstream and transition from the tents and into the hearts and the minds of the masses; 2) block the repression of the movement by protecting the right of the 99 percent's freedom of assembly and right to speak without being violently attacked; and 3) end corporate personhood. The three goals overlap and are interdependent.

We are interested in learning what your position is on mainstream filtering, the repression of civil liberties, and the role of money and politics as they relate to Occupy and the future of America.

Coverage of Occupy has been mixed. At first it was dismissive, making fun of people involved as if they were just silly kids playing games and so on. But coverage changed. In fact, one of the really remarkable and almost spectacular successes of the Occupy movement is that it has simply changed the entire framework of discussion of many issues. There were things that were sort of known, but in the margins, hidden, which are now right up front—like the imagery of the 99 percent and 1 percent; and the dramatic facts of sharply rising inequality over the past roughly thirty years, with wealth being concentrated in actually a small fraction of 1 percent of the population. This has made a very heavy impact on the ridiculous maldistribution of wealth.

For the majority, real incomes have pretty much stagnated, sometimes declined. Benefits have also declined and work hours have gone up, and so on. It's not Third World misery, but it's not what it ought to be in a rich society, the richest in the world, in fact, with plenty of wealth around, which people can see, just not in their pockets.

All of this has now been brought to the fore. You can say that it's now almost a standard framework of discussion. Even the terminology is accepted. That's a big shift.

Earlier this month, the Pew Foundation released one of its annual polls surveying what people think is the greatest source of tension and conflict in American life. For the first time ever, concern over income inequality was way at the top. It's not that the poll measured income inequality itself, but the degree to which public recognition, comprehension and understanding of the issue has gone up. That's a tribute to the Occupy movement which put this strikingly critical fact of modern life on the agenda so that people who may have known of it from their own personal experience see that they are not alone, that this is all of us. In fact, the U.S. is off the spectrum on this. The inequalities have risen to historically unprecedented heights. In the words of the first lines of the report: "The Occupy Wall Street movement no longer occupies Wall Street, but the issue of class conflict has captured a growing share of the national consciousness. A new Pew Research Center survey of 2,048 adults finds that about two-thirds of the public (66%) believes there are 'very strong' or 'strong' conflicts between the rich and the poor—an increase of 19 percentage points since 2009. Not only have perceptions of class conflict grown more prevalent; so, too, has the belief that these disputes are intense."*

Meanwhile, coverage of the Occupy movement itself has been varied. In some places, for example, parts of the business press, there has been fairly sympathetic coverage occasionally. Of course, the general picture has been: "Why don't they go home and let us get on with our work?"

* Rich Morin, "Rising Share of Americans See Conflict Between Rich and Poor," Pew Research Center, January 11, 2012.

"Where is their political program?" "How do they fit into the mainstream structure of how things are supposed to change?" And so on.

And then came the repression, which of course was inevitable. It was pretty clearly coordinated across the country. Some of it was brutal, other places less so, and there's been kind of a stand-off. Some occupations have, in effect, been removed. Others have filtered back in some other form. Some of the things have been covered, like the use of pepper spray, and so on. But a lot of it, again, is just "why don't they go away and leave us alone?" That's to be anticipated.

The question of how to respond to it—the primary way is one of the points that you made: reaching out to bring into the general Occupation, in a metaphorical sense, to bring in much wider sectors of the population. There is a lot of sympathy for the goals and aims of the Occupy movement. They're quite high in polls, in fact. But that's a big step short from engaging people in it. It has to become part of their lives, something they think they can do something about. So it's necessary to get out to where people live. That means not just sending a message, but if possible, and it would be hard, to try to spread and deepen one of the real achievements of the movement which doesn't get discussed that much in the media—at least I haven't seen it. One of the main achievements has been to create communities, real functioning communities of mutual support, democratic interchange, care for one another, and so on. This is highly significant, especially in a society like ours in which people tend to be very isolated and neighborhoods are broken down, community structures have broken down, people are kind of alone.

There's an ideology that takes a lot of effort to implant: it's so inhuman that it's hard to get into people's heads, the ideology to just take care of yourself and forget about anyone else. An extreme version is the Ayn Rand version. Actually, there's been an effort for 150 years, literally, to try to impose that way of thinking on people.

During the onset of the Industrial Revolution in Eastern Massachusetts, mid-nineteenth century, there happened to be a very lively press run by working people, young women in the factories, artisans in the mills, and so on. They had their own press that was very interesting, very widely read and had a lot of support. And they bitterly condemned the way the industrial system was taking away their freedom and liberty and imposing on them rigid hierarchical structures that they didn't want. One of their main complaints was what they called "the new spirit of the age: gain wealth forgetting all but self." For 150 years there have been massive efforts to try to impose "the new spirit of the age" on people. But it's so inhuman that there's a lot of resistance, and it continues.

One of the real achievements of the Occupy movement, I think, has been to develop a real manifestation of rejection of this in a very striking way. The people involved are not in it for themselves. They're in it for one another, for the broader society and for future generations. The bonds and associations being formed, if they can persist and if they can be brought into the wider community, would be the real defense against the inevitable repression with its sometimes violent manifestations.

How best do you think the Occupy movement should go about engaging in these, what methods should be employed, and do you think it would be prudent to actually have space to decentralize bases of operation, at least within New York City, the five boroughs?

It would certainly make sense to have spaces, whether they should be open public spaces or not. To what extent they should be is a kind of a tactical decision that has to be made on the basis of a close evaluation of circumstances, the degree of support, the degree of opposition. They're different for different places, and I don't know of any general statement.

As for methods, people in this country have problems and concerns, and if they can be helped to feel that these problems and concerns are part of a broader movement of people who support them and who they support, well then it can take off. There is no single way of doing it. There is no one answer.

You might go into a neighborhood and find that their concerns may be as simple as a traffic light on the street where kids cross to go to school. Or maybe their concerns are to prevent people from being tossed out of their homes on foreclosures. Or maybe it's to try to develop community-based enterprises, which are not at all inconceivable— enterprises owned and managed by the work force and the community which can then overcome the choice of some remote multinational and board of directors made out of banks to shift production somewhere else. These are real, very live issues happening all the time. And it can be done. Actually, a lot of it is being done in scattered ways.

A whole range of other things can be done, like addressing police brutality and civic corruption. The reconstruction of media so that it comes right out of the communities, is perfectly possible. People can have a live media system that's community-based, ethnic-based, labor-based and other groupings. All of that can be done. It takes work and it can bring people together.

Actually, I've seen things done in various places that are models of what could be followed. I'll give you an example. I happened to be in Brazil a couple of years ago and I was spending some time with Lula, the former president of Brazil, but this was before he was elected president. He was a labor activist. We traveled around together. One day he took me out to a suburb of Rio. The suburbs of Brazil are where most of the poor people live. The rich people live downtown. The suburbs don't have very much, but there are millions of people.

They have semi-tropical weather there, and the evening Lula took me out there were a lot of people in the public square. Around 9:00 p.m., prime TV time, a small group of media professionals from the town had set up a truck in the middle of the square. Their truck had a TV screen above it that presented skits and plays written and acted by people in the community. Some of them were for fun, but others addressed serious issues like debt and AIDS. As people gathered in the square, the actors walked around with microphones asking people to comment on the material that had been presented. They were filmed commenting and were shown on the screen for other people to see it. People sitting in a small bar nearby or walking in the streets began reacting, and in no time you had interesting interchanges and discussions among people about quite serious topics, topics that are part of their lives.

Well, if it can be done in a poor Brazilian slum, we can certainly do it in many other places. I'm not suggesting we do just that, but these are the kinds of things that can be done to engage broader sectors and give people a reason to feel that they can be a part of the formation of communities and the development of serious programs adapted to whatever the serious needs happen to be.

From very simple things up to starting a new socio-economic system with worker and community-run enterprises, a whole range of things is possible. I don't think there's any particular formula to go about doing it any more than there has been in any other popular movement. With a little imagination, initiative and engagement, I think many such possibilities are opened up and that's a means of defense. The more active public support there is the better defense there is against repression and violence.

How would you go about dealing with the daunting task of getting money out of politics? And can you see that happening as an extension of the community involvement and engagement that you were just talking about?

Getting money out of politics is a very crucial matter; it has been for a long time. It's gotten much more extreme now. For a long time, elections have just been public relations extravaganzas where people are mobilized every four years to get excited to go push a button and then go home and forget about it. There are a lot of ways to go about overcoming that; some reach as far as organizing for constitutional conventions in order to take away corporate personhood. We're not anywhere near that. There are a bunch of more short-term things that are possible.

We happen to be in a primary period right now. The way primaries are carried out in the United States is radically undemocratic, and this is just taken for granted. Candidates show up to a town—lots of publicity, a lot of ads and so on. They then tell the people in the town, "Here's who I am, here's what I'm going to do." Of course they don't say much. And if they do say anything no one has a reason to believe them.

It's possible to imagine a primary that is done democratically. As I mentioned to Occupy Boston, the people in the town would get together, have town meetings and discussions and come up with some ideas about what they think ought to be done in the locality, in the country, foreign policy, the whole range. They might just pick their own candidates; or, if there are national candidates running, they could say, "You can come to visit us if you'd like, but we don't want to hear speeches from you. We're going to tell you what we think policy ought to be. And if you can convince us that you'll accept these policies and carry them forward, then maybe we'll vote for you." Either that or direct representation coming out of the communities would be a democratic alternative to the farcical system that we simply take for granted.

There are many other possibilities of getting money out of politics, broader ways that involve legislation and so on. These things are not in conflict with one another. There are lots of ways of going about the same ends and they are a very critical part. It's not just elections.

Things have reached a point in the United States where, even within Congress, if someone wants a position with a degree of power and authority, they literally have to buy it. It used to be that committee chairs were granted by a political party on the basis of seniority, service and other factors. Now, you literally have to pay the party to be a candidate for a chair. Well, that has an effect, too; it drives members of Congress into the same pockets if they want to get anywhere. Again, this is not 100 percent, but these are pretty widespread tendencies and are tending to fragment whatever is left of functioning democracy. You can see it in the campaigns that are just farcical.

Considering that the movement began with a relatively large dose of anarchist inspiration, how do you think we can best recapture the meaning of that term in society and dispel all the various stereotypes that exist?

To dispel the stereotypes you have to be doing something concrete and constructive that people can identify with. So, in fact, the spontaneous development of communities of mutual support and democratic participation is something that people can comprehend, and it can be considered to be a value for themselves which they can maybe develop in some other way in their own communities. That's the only way to get rid of stereotypes and develop your own conceptions of what a meaningful system of liberty and mutual aid would be like. You learn these things by doing them, and others will be brought in to the extent they see something valuable in it.

How do you assess the goals of the Democratic Party as far as co-opting the movement and what should we be vigilant and looking out for?

The Republican Party abandoned the pretense of being a political party years ago. They are committed, so uniformly and with such dedication, to tiny sectors of power and profit that they're hardly a political party any more. They have a catechism they have to repeat like a caricature of the old Communist Party. They have to do something to get a voting constituency. Of course, they can't get it from the 1 percent, to use the imagery, so they've been mobilizing sectors of the population that were always there, but not politically organized very well—religious evangelicals, nativists who are terrified that their rights and country are being taken away, and so on.

The Democrats are a little bit different and have different constituencies, but they're following pretty much the same path as the Republican Party. The centrist Democrats of today, the ones who essentially run the party, are pretty much the moderate Republicans of a generation ago and they are now kind of the mainstream of the Democratic Party. They are going to try to organize and mobilize—co-opt if you like—the constituency that's in their interest. They have pretty much abandoned the white working-class; it's rather striking to see. So that's barely part of their constituency at this point, which is a pretty sad development. They will try to mobilize Hispanics, Blacks and progressives. They'll try to reach out to the Occupy movement.

Organized labor is still part of the Democratic constituency and they'll try to co-opt them; and with Occupy, it's just the same as all the others. The political leadership will pat them on the head and say, "I'm for you, vote for me." The people involved will have to understand that maybe they'll do something for you, that only if you maintain substantial pressure can you get elected leadership to do things—but they're not going to do it on their own, with very rare exceptions.

As far as money and politics are concerned, it's hard to beat the comment of the great political financier, Mark Hanna. About a century ago, he was asked what was important in politics. He answered, "The first is money, the second one is money and I've forgotten what the third one is."

That was a century ago. Today it's much more extreme. So yes, concentrated wealth will, of course, try to use its wealth and power to take over the political system as much as possible, and to run it and do what it wants, etc. It would be a miracle if it didn't. The public has to find ways to struggle against that.

Centuries ago, political theorists like David Hume, in one of his foundations for government, pointed out correctly that power is in the hands of the governed and not the governors. This is true for a feudal society, a military state or a parliamentary democracy. Power is in the hands of the governed. The only way the rulers can overcome that is by control of opinions and attitudes.

Hume was right in the mid-eighteenth century. What he said remains true today. The power is in the hands of the general population. There are massive efforts to control it by less force today because of the many rights that have been won. Methods now are by propaganda, consumerism, stirring up ethnic hatred, all kinds of ways. Sure, that will always go on but we have to find ways to resist it.

There is nothing wrong with giving tentative support to a particular candidate as long as that person is doing what you want. But it would be a more democratic society if we could also recall them without a huge effort. There are other ways of pressuring candidates. There is a fine line between doing that and being co-opted, mobilized to serve someone else's interest. But those are just constant decisions and choices that have to be made.

Could you speak a little about Antonio Gramsci, how his ideas relate to the things you've been talking about.

I like Gramsci. He's an important person. He talked about things not unlike what David Hume was saying—how cultural hegemony was established by systems of power. I personally think that his work is worth reading. When I read it, it says much of what we already know. I don't find anything novel. Maybe it's just my inadequacy; you can read it and see what you think.

A great deal of our economics is dominated by the idea of more and more growth.

The whole human species currently faces a very serious problem of whether even decent existence can be carried forward. We are coming close to the edge of a precipice of environmental destruction. If growth is understood and accepted to include constant attacks on the physical environment that sustains life—like, for example, greenhouse emissions, destruction of agricultural land, and so forth—if that's what it means, then we are like lemmings walking over a cliff. This isn't what growth has to mean. For example, growth can mean simpler lives and more livable communities. It takes work and doesn't just come by itself. It takes labor and development of a different kind. Part of what functioning, free communities like the Occupy communities can be working for and spreading to others is just a different way of living, which is not based on maximizing consumer goods, but on maximizing values that are important for life. That's growth, too, just growth in a different direction.

Can you talk about the most recent crisis of the real estate bubble, how we got to this point in terms of historical context, why you think it occurred and what was at the root of its occurrence?

At the root of its occurrence is the major shift in the economy that began to take place in the 1970s. It was escalated radically under Reagan, Thatcher in England and on from there. There was a big growth period in the United States, the largest in history, during the 1950s and 1960s. At that time, there was also egalitarianism: the lowest quintile did as well as the highest quintile and it absorbed into the mainstream society. Groups that had been excluded from society, African Americans for example, could finally be integrated into society. That came to an end in the 1970s when, for one thing, there was a shift towards increasing the role of finance in the society.

One of the great financial correspondents, Martin Wolf, wrote recently that the financial systems are wiping out functioning markets the way larva destroys a host. He's one of the most respected financial economists in the world and not a radical. That's what the effect of the financial system has been. Combined with this were corporate decisions to ship production abroad. It's not a law of nature, again. You can have decent working conditions and production at home and abroad, but they made more profit that way. These decisions greatly changed the economy. One effect of this was that wealth became concentrated heavily in financial industries and that led to concentration of political power that leads to legislation, so on and so forth, keeping the vicious cycle going.

Part of this was deregulation. During the 1950s and 1960s, the great growth period, the banks were regulated and there was no crisis. No major bubbles burst. Starting in the 1980s, you started getting financial crises, bubbles. There were several during the Reagan administrations. The Clinton administration ended with a huge tech-bubble burst.

There is a lot of money floating around, and much less real production that people need. One of the ways in which households were able to survive during the period of stagnation was just by getting caught up in bubbles. Early in this century, housing prices started to shoot up way beyond the trend. There is a kind of trend line for about a century. Housing prices roughly match gross domestic product. About ten years ago, they just started shooting way out of sight, with no fundamentals. A lot of it was essentially robbery: subprime mortgages and complicated devices by which the banks could slice up mortgages so that others would have responsibility when it collapsed, complicated derivatives and other financial instruments. All of this took off and created a huge bubble that was obviously going to burst. It was barely even noticed by the entire economist profession, including the Federal Reserve.

The minutes of the 2006 Federal Reserve

meeting came out recently, you might have seen them. And rather strikingly, there was no recognition there that there was a multi-trillion dollar housing bubble that had no basis whatsoever and was going to collapse. As a matter of fact, they were congratulating themselves on how marvelously they were running the economy. Well, of course, it collapsed as it had to, maybe 8 trillion dollars lost.

For much of the population, that's all they had. Many African Americans' net worth was practically reduced to nothing, and many others, too. It's a disaster. This kind of thing is going to happen as long as you have unregulated capital markets, which furthermore have a government insurance policy. It's called "too big to fail": if you get in trouble, the taxpayer will bail you out—policies that, of course, lead to underestimation of risk.

Credit agencies already take into account the fact that it's going to be rescued next time it goes bust. Well, that of course increases risk even further. If not housing, it'll be something else, commodities or whatever.

It's a financial casino instead of a protected economy, and of course people get hurt who are not rich and powerful, the 99 percent.

2ND TIME IVE
FOUGHT FOR
MY COUNTRY
1ST TIME
IVE KNOWN
MY ENEMY

OCCUPYING FOREIGN POLICY

University of Maryland Friday, January 27, 2012

How do we occupy the foreign-policy establishment?

The same way you bring about other changes. By comparative standards, the United States remains a very free country. You get a lot of opportunities. They range from electoral politics to demonstrations, resistance and organizing public pressure. That's the way you do it.

In fact, you don't have to go very far. The educational establishment, the intellectual establishment, is up to their neck in this. And we live right in the middle of it. Of course, that can be influenced, you know, in classrooms and writing and organization and all sorts of things.

I hear the question often and I don't really understand it. In the United States we can do almost anything we want. It's not like Egypt, where you're going to get murdered by the security forces. Here, there's some repression sometimes: but by international standards, by comparative standards, it's so slight that it hardly counts, certainly for privileged people—not for poor people. They can get it in the neck. But for those with privilege, the opportunities are just overwhelming. There's nothing to stop all kinds of action, from education and organizing to political action, to demonstrations. All kinds of resistance are possible, the kinds of things that have succeeded in the past.

After all, we have a history of success in getting policy changes. The New Deal legislation, for example, didn't come out of nowhere. That came out of very large-scale popular activism, which reached the point where the business world and the government agreed to allow progressive legislation to pass. The business world quickly tried to undermine it, but they had to accept it. By the time sit-down strikes were taking place, the business world could easily see that the next step is just taking over the factory, running it, and kicking them out. Well, they didn't want to allow that, so some legislation, important legislation passed. And under other massive popular organization and pressure, other things happened.

Similar things have happened since. In the 1960s, for example, the antiwar movement, which I mentioned, it got from essentially nowhere to a strong mass popular movement by 1968. If you read the Pentagon Papers, one of the most interesting sections is the final section, which ends in

mid-1968. If you take a look at that section, you'll
see that during the first few months of 1968, the
president wanted to send hundreds of thousands
more troops to South Vietnam. The military and
the Joint Chiefs were opposed because they said
that they would need the troops for civil disorder
control in the United States. The population was
just going to get out of control—young people,
women, minorities, others. They knew that they
would need the troops to control the population
here so they didn't send them. Well, you know,
when the government gets that wary, you've had
an effect. They did other horrible things—clan-
destine things that could've been worse, but it
was bad enough, like I mentioned.

Actually, the same thing happened in the Iraq
War. The protests against the Iraq War were historically totally unique. I think it's the first war
in history where there was massive protest before
the war was officially launched. I can't think of a
case where that ever happened. And it's claimed
that the protests had no effect, but I don't think
that's true. It should have gone on. Unfortu-
nately, it reduced, and that allowed more leeway
for aggression.

But the Iraq War was nothing like the war
against South Vietnam. The policies that Kennedy
and Johnson routinely carried out without even
thinking about it were never tried in Iraq. There

was no chemical warfare, there was no saturation bombing by B-52s, there was no—what are called "population control measures"—where you drive the population into concentration camps. None of those measures were even tried. And I think one reason they weren't tried was because it was understood that the public was not going to tolerate them this time. So, okay, it had a kind of a retarding effect.

There are other kinds of popular organization that have had major effects. The country is a much more civilized place now than it was in the 1960s in many respects. Take, for example, women's rights. In the 1960s, women literally still were not guaranteed the right to serve on juries. They'd won the right to vote forty years before, but by the 1960s, in many states, they couldn't serve on juries. In 1960, my university was almost 100 percent white male. Now it's much more diverse and that's the case over much of the country.

Well, that's a big change in the nature of the society and the culture. It didn't happen by magic. It wasn't a gift from above. It came from extensive organizing activities and corresponding actions which finally broke down a lot of barriers and freed things up. That's the way changes take place. And all those methods are still available.

I was wondering if you have read Gar Alperovitz's

book America Beyond Capitalism, *and if you have, what you thought of his ideas in the book.*

It's a very important book, and the work that's described there is extremely important. The book reviews work that Alperovitz has been involved in for some years in trying to develop worker-owned enterprises, mostly in Ohio. That's one of the things that can be done. It's very feasible.

Actually, if you could take a look at standard texts in business economics—you know, nothing radical—standard texts in business economics point out that there's no economic principle or any other principle that says that *shareholders* should have a higher priority than *stakeholders*—workers and community. Shareholders, incidentally, doesn't mean somebody whose pension fund has two dollars as a share. Shareholders are very narrowly concentrated, the top 1 percent of the population, and that means big banks, interlocking directorates, and so on. There's no economic principle that says they are the ones who should determine investment policy, like shipping production to Foxconn. There's no law of economics that says that has to happen. It could just as well be done by stakeholders, by the workforce and the community—perfectly consistent with anything that anyone claims about economic theory.

There's no reason for the Occupy movement to be less imaginative and ambitious than standard business texts. So, yes, stakeholders could take over parts of the economy that are being dismantled, run them effectively, and direct them to different purposes. These are very feasible tasks.

So, for example, one of the things that Obama is praised for by left-liberal economists, Paul Krugman and others, is for having essentially nationalized the auto industry and reconstructed it. That's pretty much what happened. Well, once the auto industry was nationalized, there were alternatives. And one alternative was to reconstruct it and hand it back to the original owners— not to the same names, but to the same class, the same banks, and so on. That's what was done. Another possibility would have been to hand the auto industry over to the workforce and the communities, the stakeholders, and redirect it towards things that the country really needs.

These are the kinds of things that Gar Alperovitz is talking about, feasible things that could have a big effect on the society. And Alperovitz is one of the very few people who is really doing very good work on this. His book is certainly worth reading and thinking about what it describes and what options it suggests.

Examples come up all the time. Here's one from a place near where I live. About a year ago in Taunton, a manufacturing town outside of Boston, there was a small, reasonably successful manufacturing plant. It was producing high-tech equipment for aircraft, and it apparently was doing okay; but it wasn't making enough profit for the managers and the multinational corporation that owned it. So the corporation wanted to just dismantle it. The United Electrical Workers Union wanted to buy the operation and run it themselves, but the corporation wouldn't agree. I suspect that it wouldn't agree mostly on class grounds: it's not a good idea to let people own and manage their own workplaces—people might get the wrong idea. Anyhow, whatever the reason, it didn't work.

But if the Occupy movement had been around back then and had been active and energetic enough and had reached out sufficiently, that's the kind of thing it could have participated in and supported; and maybe it could have helped the workers gain the edge they needed to win. These are the kinds of options that are all over the place right now, ones that support from a movement can really impact.

AUDIENCE: Can we get a question from a woman?

M.C.: Fair enough. Thank you—.

WOMAN FROM THE AUDIENCE: I am an adjunct professor, what's known as a "Beltway adjunct." I teach eight classes a semester, and I have no health insurance and no retirement benefits. I'm a communications scholar, and I've studied your work for the last fifteen years. And I want to know, beyond the critique—which was a marvelous critique, by the way, thank you—what are the discursive strategies that we can use to combat the ideologically driven discourse that dominates the politics that we deal with in the classroom and beyond every day? I know I have friends, colleagues, and family members who are staunch supporters of the Republican worldview, and it's hard to have meaningful dialogues with them. Facts no longer seem to matter. That being the case, how do we begin to talk about truth in a meaningful way? What kind of linguistic strategies do we use to drive change?

Just about every talk I give, the same question comes up: how about allowing a question from a woman? Why does that question even arise? We don't ask the question, "How about allowing a question from somebody with blonde hair?" Why is the discrimination so deeply embedded, and in fact internalized, that we still have to raise the question? And it's uniform. I can't remember a talk where this didn't come up. So that's something to think about. That's still a battle to be won internally and in the society.

As far as the discursive strategies are concerned, I don't think there are any answers other than the ones we all know, the ones that have succeeded—not 100 percent, of course. Every success is limited. There are failures. But there are successes.

There are things practically everybody can do, and if you are from a privileged sector of the population, then there are even more opportunities. You can speak, you can write, you can organize, you can reach out to other people. If you keep doing it, it can have an impact.

Take a case like the women's movement. I mean, a lot of you are old enough to remember how that happened. It began with very small consciousness-raising groups—groups of women getting together and talking to each other and coming to identify and comprehend that, first of all there is oppression, and that a better way is possible where we don't have to accept oppression. If you had asked my grandmother if she was oppressed, she wouldn't have known what you were talking about. Of course, she was hopelessly oppressed, but identifying it is not always easy, especially if no one talks about it. So just getting to understand that you don't have to accept oppression, that you can be a free and independent person, is a big step. The women's movement took that step and kept going. There was bitter resistance; it wasn't easy by any means. And, in fact, there still is, and there's a backlash, and so on and so forth. But you just keep struggling for it.

The civil rights movement didn't get anywhere near Martin Luther King's dream, but it did bring big change. Things are still bad, but not like they were in Alabama in 1960. The organizing goes back decades, of course, but it really took off when a couple of young black students sat in at a lunch counter about sixty-one years ago. Pretty soon, the SNCC formed, the Student Nonviolent Coordinating Committee. The students got some support in Spelman College in Atlanta, where a lot of the SNCC activists came from. There were two faculty members who supported them— Howard Zinn and Staughton Lynd—and both got expelled. But they did get some support. And the Freedom Riders' bus trips started. There was a little participation from the North.

Repression against the movement was very brutal. People were beaten and killed. You know, not fun. I mean, I remember demonstrations in 1965, in the South, where the police violence was brutal and federal marshals stood around, kind of watching them, not doing anything.

Things hit a limit as soon as they reached the North. It's striking. In 1966, Martin Luther King expanded the movement to Chicago; then they were just dumped on miserably. It was an effort to mobilize people, starting with the poor, around the issue of slums. When they moved on to criticize the war in Vietnam, there was huge antagonism against them. They ended up the way I described, mostly written out of history by Northern liberals. But they did have successes, and the successes are real, and we know how they were won.

Same with everything else. For example, the Vietnam War protests did reach a substantial level, but remember what it was like for years. When I started giving talks about the Vietnam War in the early 1960s, they were usually held in somebody's living room or in a church with four or five people attending. And in fact, if we tried to do it at the college, MIT, you'd have to bring together half a dozen topics and make one of them Vietnam in the hope that somebody would show up. As late as October 1965 in Boston, which is a liberal city, you could not have a public demonstration against the war, literally. It would be violently broken up, often by students. It's a fact.

By March 1966, there were hundreds of thousands of U.S. troops rampaging in South Vietnam, destroying huge parts of the country. Since we couldn't have public demonstrations in Boston without their getting broken up, we tried to have one in a church downtown. As a result of our event, the church was attacked, defaced with tomatoes and cans. A police contingent was sent. I walked outside and stood next to the police captain and asked him, "Can't you do something to stop the defacing of the church?" And he said, no, he couldn't do anything. A moment later, a tomato hit him in the face, and in about thirty seconds the place was cleared. A year later, there were big demonstrations.

And there were no special strategies or tricks leading up to the demonstrations, just what we all know how to do. If people don't want to think about what's going on, try to bring up the importance of understanding facts. In fact, if you look at public attitudes, even Tea Party attitudes, they're kind of social-democratic, literally. So, for example, among Tea Party advocates and, of course, the rest of the population, a considerable majority are in favor of more spending for health and more spending for education. They're against welfare, but more spending to help, say, women with dependent children.

That's the result of very effective propaganda. One of Ronald Reagan's great successes was to demonize the concept of welfare. In Reaganite rhetoric, welfare means a rich black woman driving to a welfare office in a chauffeured Cadillac so she can take your hard-earned money and spend it on drugs or something. Well, nobody's in favor of that. But are you in favor of what welfare actually does? Yeah, that ought to supported.

The same is true on health, on the deficit and the other things I mentioned. I think it's two-thirds of the population that thinks that corporations should be deprived of personal rights. If that were to be enacted, it would be a pretty significant move. It would undo a century of court decisions. It's not just Citizens United. It goes back a century. And that's against the will of about two-thirds of the population. Well, all these things offer plenty of opportunities for discussion, interchange, education, organizing and activism. The opportunities are all there.

TO BE HOPEFUL in bad times is not just foolishly romantic. It is based on the fact that human history is a history not only of cruelty, but also of compassion, sacrifice, courage, kindness.

What we choose to emphasize in this complex history will determine our lives. If we see only the worst, it destroys our capacity to do something. If we remember those times and places—and there are so many—where people have behaved magnificently, this gives us the energy to act, and at least the possibility of sending this spinning top of a world in a different direction.

And if we do act, in however small a way, we don't have to wait for some grand utopian future. The future is an infinite succession of presents, and to live now as we think human beings should live, in defiance of all that is bad around us, is itself a marvelous victory.*

—HOWARD ZINN

* Howard Zinn, *You Can't be Neutral on A Moving Train*, Beacon Press, Beacon Press, 1994; Howard Zinn, *A Power Governments Cannot Suppress*, City Lights, 2007.

REMEMBERING HOWARD ZINN

It is not easy for me to write a few words about Howard Zinn, the great American activist and historian. He was a very close friend for forty-five years. The families were very close, too. His wife, Roz, who died of cancer not long before, was also a marvelous person and close friend. Also somber is the realization that a whole generation seems to be disappearing, including several other old friends: Edward Said, Eqbal Ahmed and others, who were not only astute and productive scholars, but also dedicated and courageous militants, always on call when needed—which was constant. A combination that is essential if there is to be hope of decent survival.

Howard's remarkable life and work are summarized best in his own words. His primary concern, he explained, was "the countless small actions of unknown people" that lie at the roots of "those great moments" that enter the historical record—a record that will be profoundly misleading, and seriously disempowering, if it is torn from these roots as it passes through the filters of doctrine and dogma. His life was always closely intertwined with his writings and innumerable talks and interviews. It was devoted, selflessly, to empowerment of the unknown people who brought about great moments. That was true when he was an industrial worker and labor activist, and from the days, fifty years ago, when he was teaching at Spelman College in Atlanta, Georgia, a black college that was open mostly to the small black elite.

While teaching at Spelman, Howard supported the students who were at the cutting edge of the civil rights movement in its early and most dangerous days, many of whom became quite well-known in later years—Alice Walker, Julian Bond and others—and who loved and revered him, as did everyone who knew him well. And as always, he did not just support them, which was rare enough, but also participated directly with them in their most hazardous efforts—no easy undertaking at that time, before there was any organized popular movement and in the face of government hostility that lasted for some years. Finally, popular support was ignited, in large part by the courageous actions of the young people who were sitting in at lunch counters, riding freedom buses, organizing demonstrations, facing bitter racism and brutality, sometimes death.

By the early 1960s, a mass popular movement was taking shape, by then with Martin Luther King in a leadership role—and the government had to respond. As a reward for his courage and honesty, Howard was soon expelled from the college where he taught. A few years later, he wrote the standard work on SNCC (the Student Non-violent Coordinating Committee), the major organization of those "unknown people" whose "countless small actions" played such an important part in creating the groundswell that enabled King to gain significant influence—as I am sure he would have been the first to say—and to bring the country to honor the constitutional amendments of a century earlier that had theoretically granted elementary civil rights to former slaves— at least to do so partially; no need to stress that there remains a long way to go.

A Civilizing Influence

On a personal note, I came to know Howard well when we went together to a civil rights demonstration in Jackson Mississippi in (I think) 1964, even at that late date, a scene of violent public antagonism, police brutality and indifference—or even cooperation—with state security forces on the part of federal authorities, sometimes in ways that were quite shocking. After being expelled from the

Atlanta college where he taught, Howard came to
Boston, and spent the rest of his academic career
at Boston University, where he was, I am sure,
the most admired and loved faculty member on
campus, and the target of bitter antagonism and
petty cruelty on the part of the administration. In
later years, however, after his retirement, he gained
the public honor and respect that was always overwhelming among students, staff, much of the
faculty, and the general community. While there,
Howard wrote the books that brought him well-
deserved fame. His book *Logic of Withdrawal*, in
1967, was the first to express clearly and power-
fully what many were then beginning barely to
contemplate: that the United States had no right
even to call for a negotiated settlement in Vietnam,
leaving Washington with power and substantial
control in the country it had invaded and had by
then already largely destroyed.

Rather, the United States should do what any
aggressor should: withdraw; allow the population to somehow reconstruct as they could from
the wreckage; and, if minimal honesty could be
attained, pay massive reparations for the crimes
that the invading armies had committed, vast
crimes in this case. The book had wide influence
among the public, although to this day, its message
can barely even be comprehended in elite educated
circles, an indication of how much necessary work

lies ahead. Significantly, among the general public by the war's end, 70 per cent regarded the war as "fundamentally wrong and immoral," not "a mistake," a remarkable figure, considering the fact that scarcely a hint of such a thought was expressible in mainstream opinion. Howard's writings—and, as always, his prominent presence in protest and direct resistance—were a major factor in civilizing much of the country.

In those same years, Howard also became one of the most prominent supporters of the resistance movement that was then developing. He was one of the early signers of the Call to Resist Illegitimate Authority and was so close to the activities of Resist that he was practically one of the organizers. He also took part at once in the sanctuary actions that had a remarkable impact in galvanizing anti-war protest. Whatever was needed—talks, participation in civil disobedience, support for resisters, testimony at trials—Howard was always there.

History from Below

Even more influential in the long run than Howard's anti-war writings and actions was his enduring masterpiece, *A People's History of the United States*, a book that literally changed the consciousness of a generation. Here he developed with care, lucidity and comprehensive sweep his fundamental message about the crucial role of the people who remain unknown in carrying forward the endless struggle for peace and justice, and about the victims of the systems of power that create their own versions of history and seek to impose it. Later, his *Voices of the People's History*, now an acclaimed theatrical and television production, brought to many the actual words of those forgotten or ignored people who have played such a valuable role in creating a better world.

Howard's unique success in drawing the actions and voices of unknown people from the depths to which they had largely been consigned has spawned extensive historical research following a similar path, focusing on critical periods of U.S. history, and turning to the record in other countries as well, a very welcome development. It is not entirely novel—there had been scholarly inquiries of particular topics before—but nothing to compare with Howard's broad and incisive evocation of "history from below," compensating for critical omissions in how U.S. history had been interpreted and conveyed. Howard's dedicated activism continued, literally without a break, until the very end, even in his last years, when he was suffering from severe infirmity and personal loss—though one would hardly know it when meeting him or watching him speaking tirelessly to captivated audiences all over the country. Whenever there was a struggle for peace and justice, Howard was there, on the front lines, unflagging in his enthusiasm, and inspiring in his integrity, engagement, eloquence and insight; a light touch of humor in the face of adversity; and dedication to non-violence and sheer decency. It is hard even to imagine how many young people's lives were touched, and how deeply, by his achievements, both in his work and his life. There are places where Howard's life and work should have particular resonance. One, which should be much better known, is Turkey. I know of no other country where leading writers, artists, journalists, academics and other intellectuals have compiled such an impressive record of bravery and integrity in condemning crimes of the state, and going beyond to engage in civil disobedience to try to bring oppression and violence to an end, facing and sometimes enduring severe repression, and then returning to the task.

It is an honorable record, unique to my knowledge, a record of which the country should be proud. And one that should be a model for others, just as Howard Zinn's life and work are an unforgettable model, sure to leave a permanent stamp on how history is understood and how a decent and honorable life should be lived.

OCCUPY PROTEST SUPPORT

Advice for Occupy protesters in the US, by NATIONAL LAWYERS GUILD

Thousands of people have been arrested exercising their freedom of speech and assembly while participating in Occupy actions. If you or someone you know needs legal assistance or has been the victim of excessive police force or brutality at a protest or gathering, contact the National Lawyers Guild, a non-profit federation of lawyers, legal workers and law students who join in at Occupy protests and monitor police activity on the street and in jail. The Guild has been providing invaluable legal advice to movement folks who get inadvertently arrested at protests, as well as those who consciously commit civil disobedience.

"What laws and police practices should I know about?"

You have First Amendment rights to protest lawfully. You have the right to hand out leaflets, rally on a sidewalk, and set up a moving picket line, so long as you do not block building entrances or more than half the sidewalk. The law requires a permit to march in the street, rally in a park with 20 or more people, or use electronic sound amplification. In New York, a "Mask Law" makes it unlawful for three or more people to wear masks, including bandanas: the NYPD aggressively enforces this law. Police will seize signs on wooden sticks, metal, and pvc piping—it's OK to attach signs to cardboard tubing. The police will not allow placing signs on fences or trees. If you hang a banner from a bridge over a highway, you risk arrest for Reckless Endangerment.

"What do I do if the police talk to me?"

You have a constitutional right to remain silent. If the police try a friendly conversation, you can say nothing and walk away. If the police say, "MOVE!" or give some other order, you may ask, "Why?" but you are advised not to say anything more. Notify a Legal Observer about the order. If the police ask to search you or your bag, you should say, "NO, I do not consent to a search." If the police search anyway, you are advised to continue to say, "I do not consent to a search." If you physically interfere with the search, you risk arrest. If the police question you, including asking your name, you may say nothing and walk away. If the police prevent you from leaving, ask, "Am I free to go?" If they answer "YES," you may say nothing and walk away. If they answer "NO," say, "I wish to remain silent. I want to talk to a lawyer," and wait for the police to arrest or release you.

"What can I do to prepare for a possible arrest?"

Write the Guild's phone number on your wrist or ankle; call this if you are arrested or if you see an arrest. Carry in your pocket several quarters to make telephone calls and a phone card for possible long distance calls. Carry a granola bar in your pocket; food is often missed in jail. Carry in your pocket one photo ID with a good address; do not carry ID with different addresses. Do not carry anything you do not want the police to have such as phone books or valuables.

"What do I do if I get arrested?"

You are advised to state clearly, "I am going to remain silent. I want to speak to a lawyer." Repeat this to any officer who questions you. Do not believe everything the police say—it is legal for the police to lie to you to get you to talk. When asked, you can give your name and address, show photo ID, and allow yourself to be photographed and fingerprinted for purposes of confirming ID; refusal to provide ID information will delay your release from jail. Remember your arresting officer's name and badge number. If you get to a phone, call the NLG and give names of other arrestees. Remain calm and prepare yourself for a possible wait in jail for 24–36 hours.

"What will happen to me if I am arrested?"

You will be handcuffed and driven to a jail or detention center and later taken to court. In the police's discretion, you may be released from jail with a summons or desk appearance ticket ("DAT"), which tells you when to return to court. If you are charged with a misdemeanor or felony, you will more likely "go through the system" to be arraigned before a judge—this means you will be in jail for 24 to 36 hours. Don't talk to anyone but a lawyer about the facts of your arrest. A court employee will interview you about community ties (address, employment, family) to help the judge determine whether to set bail or release you on your own recognizance ("ROR"); it's OK to answer these questions—just don't talk about your arrest. A lawyer will briefly meet you about your case. Get the lawyer's name and phone number. You will be arraigned on the charges against you before a judge. Your lawyer will enter your pleas; when in doubt, plead, "Not Guilty." Conditions for release are set, either bail money or ROR. The next court date is scheduled on a court slip for you to keep. You may be offered an Adjournment in Contemplation of Dismissal ("ACD"). If you agree, your case is adjourned for 6 months. If you are not arrested during the 6 months, the charge is dismissed and the case is sealed. If you are arrested during the 6 months, the case can be brought back to court. If this happens, you still have all the rights you would normally have with a criminal case, including the right to trial. An ACD is NOT a plea of "Guilty."

"What do I do if the police knock at my door?"

If anyone knocks, don't open the door. Ask "Who are you?" If it is the police ask, "What do you want?"

"We just want to talk to you." If they say they want to come in or talk with you, state: "I have nothing to say. Slide your business card under the door. My lawyer will call you." Move away from the door and call the NLG.

"We have a search warrant." You reply: "If you have a warrant, slip it under the door." If they do, read it to confirm it is the correct address; if it is, open the door, step back, and state "I am going to remain silent. I want to speak to a lawyer." A

warrant is sometimes limited to a specific room; make mental notes of where the police search. If they don't have a warrant, again reply, "I have nothing to say. Slide your business card under the door."

"We have an arrest warrant." You reply: "If you have a warrant, slip it under the door." If they do, read it to determine if it is a warrant for your arrest or for someone else. If it is for you [or someone inside], tell them you are coming out, step out and close and lock the door behind you and state "I am going to remain silent. I want to speak to a lawyer." Do not say or do anything else. If the arrest warrant is for someone not inside your home, state the person is not there (or does not live there) and ask for the police to slip a business card under the door. Do not say or do anything else.

"What if I am not a U.S. citizen?"

There are far greater risks involved if you are arrested and you are not a U.S. citizen. Talk to a lawyer before coming to a protest. Always carry the name and telephone number of an immigration lawyer. Carry any immigration papers you might have such as your "green card," I-94, or work authorization with you as well.

ABOUT ZUCCOTTI PARK PRESS AND THE OCCUPIED MEDIA PAMPHLET SERIES

Inspired by the transformation of Zuccotti Park into a liberated space for dreaming, organizing, advocacy, art, free speech and creative community, Zuccotti Park Press/Occupied Media Pamphlet Series is founded to extend that spirit through the printed word and to join in the advocacy of social change through public participation in debate, protest and genuine democracy.

Produced by Adelante Alliance, a Brooklyn-based non-profit that serves the Spanish-speaking immigrant community, the goal of the new press is to produce accessible, affordable, pamphlet-size works by well-known and emerging voices who are inspired by a vision for a new society.

Join us to celebrate the printed word, the tradition of the pamphlet and the key role that bookstores play in protecting free speech and creating community.

To quote our forthcoming pamphlet with Angela Davis, "We transform the meaning of occupation.

We turn occupation into something that is beautiful, something that brings community together, something that calls for love and happiness and hope."